YOGA
STORYTIME

BREATHE ✳ STRETCH ✳ BE CALM

YOGA
STORYTIME

MÍRIAM RAVENTÓS

ILLUSTRATIONS BY **MARIA GIRÓN**

GIBBS SMITH
TO ENRICH AND INSPIRE HUMANKIND

Can you do many things at once?

For example . . .

Can you play with a toy truck on the table while having breakfast?

Can you walk and talk while kicking a ball at the same time?

Can you sing while playing with soap bubbles in the bathtub?

Sure . . . it's not that hard, is it?

Well, many, many years ago in India, some men realized that doing many
things at one time was fairly easy, and that they could do more every day.
But they wondered what would happen if they only did one thing,
   the simplest,
            the most natural one,
                        one thing only and nothing more.

Do you have any idea what this thing was?

They decided that the simplest thing they could do was BREATHE.

You're right, breathing and walking is easy, breathing and playing even more so, and breathing and sleeping is a snap. . . . The difficult thing was just breathing, and being aware of just that and *not* getting distracted.

Try it yourself! You breathe, don't you?

The men sat on the floor, closed their eyes so they couldn't see anything, and tried to just breathe while thinking about their breathing.

It made them feel good!

You are one person. If you're with a friend, you're two people. With Dad, Mom, and your friend, that makes four people. But if the four of you sit really still, breathe quietly, and think about your breathing, you will feel like the four of you are a single person sharing only one breath.

For the men I mentioned, this discovery was very interesting. They sat and breathed, and they felt as one together and one with everything.

These men definitely agreed that one was a good number, but also that doing only *one* thing is much more difficult than doing *many* things at once.

Sit down on the floor for a little while like they did. Close your eyes.
Are you thinking about your breathing?
Count your breaths: one, two, three, four . . . count at least to ten, and then start over again—ten more.

The men from India came to realize, as you may also realize,
that doing nothing other than breathing is not easy.
Do you want to move your feet?
     Does your nose itch?
          Is your back stiff?
               Are noises bothering you?
                    Do you want to eat something?
               Do you feel like talking, or screaming?
          Do you want to play or run?

They realized that in order to do something like this they needed to train.

What did they need to train?
They needed to train their bodies so they could stand still without complaining.

And they needed to train their thoughts, since those are even busier than their bodies. They realized that thoughts move faster than a monkey bitten by a scorpion.

These men loved the world around them. There were
many things to learn.
They observed the trees, still and tireless, and they
imitated them by doing the **TREE POSE.**

They observed the moon,
sometimes growing and
other times getting small,
and copied it by doing the
HALF-MOON POSE.

They observed cats, who are so agile, and imitated them by doing the **CAT POSE** and stretching like they do.

They observed lions, so brave, strong, and confident, and they imitated them by doing the **LION POSE.**

They observed snakes, stealthy and alert, and
they imitated them by doing the **COBRA POSE.**

They observed tortoises in their shells
and saw that inside they do not feel the cold or heat, and they
imitated them by doing the **TORTOISE POSE.**

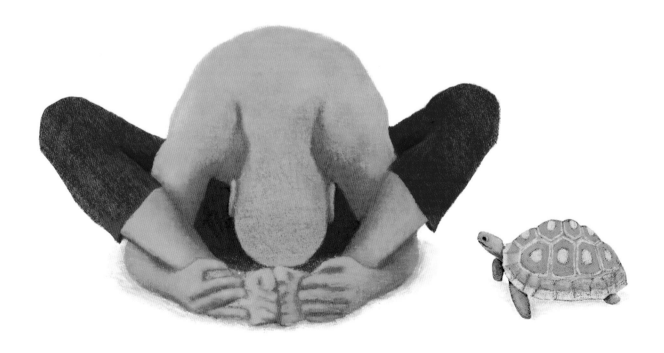

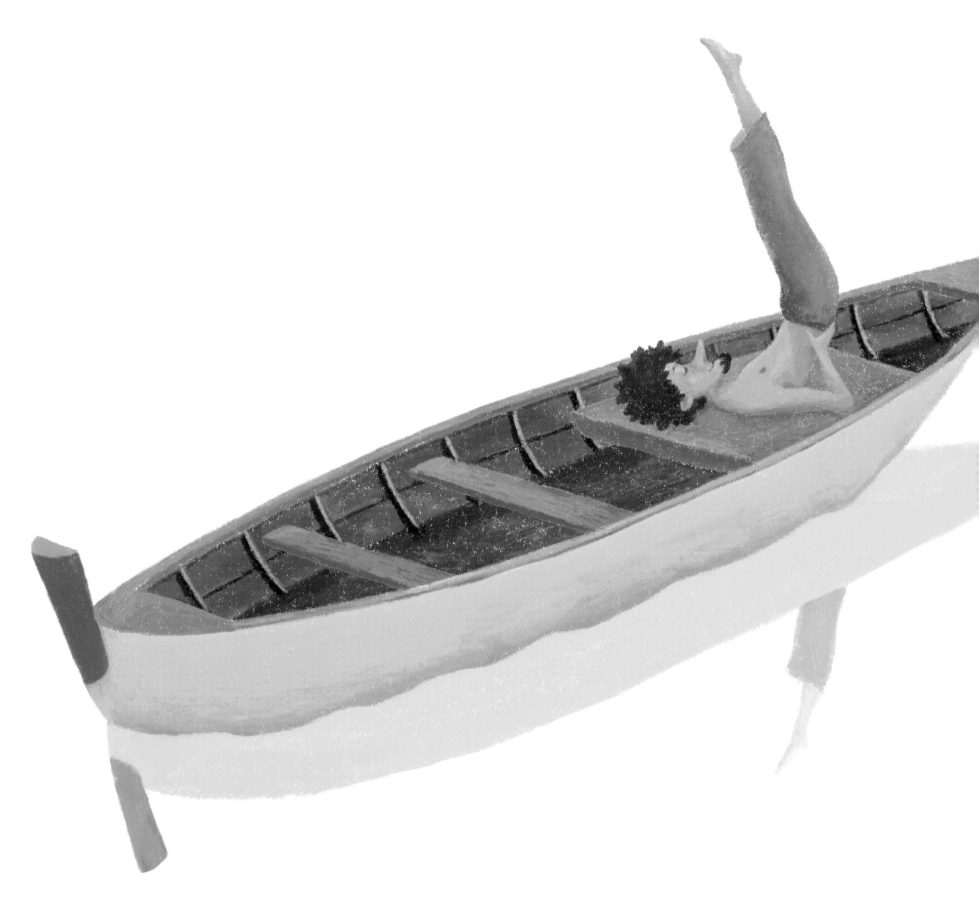

They wanted to see the world upside down.

They created many more poses and their backs became stronger and more flexible.
This way they could stay sitting and breathing for hours and hours.
And they felt more and more at ease with the world and with themselves.

In addition to training the outside of their bodies, they also took care of the inside of their bodies.

Have you ever had a stuffy nose?
Whew, how difficult it is to breathe . . .
Then they learned how to unstuff it with saltwater.

They also cleaned their intestines, their eyes, and their stomach.

They also discovered things to empty their mind of thoughts. They breathed fast and noisily when exhaling.

Or very slowly—first one nostril and then the other. And they held their breath longer than deep-sea divers!

Sit on the floor and try to empty *your* mind of thoughts. Hold your left nostril closed and breathe slowly through your right nostril. Out, then in. Now hold your right nostril closed and breathe slowly through the left one. Out, in. Do it two more times: right—out, in; left—out, in. And again.

Now, how long can you hold your breath?

The men from India were grateful for this knowledge because it made them feel better, and they sang songs of thanksgiving to the stars, to the wise men, and to the gods.

The men from India knew that these discoveries were very valuable and they didn't want them to be lost.

So they taught them to their children, who taught them to *their* children . . . and they continue to be passed down to each new generation.

This is YOGA.

So many things can be learned from being able to do just one thing:
    NOTHING MORE THAN BREATHING!

READING GUIDE

READING GUIDE

How Do You Practice Yoga?

Most yoga poses are simple and inspired by nature. Did you already notice that the poses imitate trees, animals, or celestial bodies?

I'll teach you only *some* poses; you can learn the rest of the poses later on from a teacher.

To get started, set up a safe and open space where you can practice in a familiar environment. A camping mat or other thin mat will help you protect your body when you lie down on the floor, and keep you from getting hurt if you fall. You need to have space to stretch and move.

Don't be in a hurry; you don't have to do all the poses, just the ones you want to. Repeat them more than once, and between poses always rest a little while and breathe!

Are You Breathing?

Start by blowing; pretend you're holding a balloon to your lips. Inhale, blow, and inflate your imaginary balloon as much as you can. When you can't inflate it any more, tie a knot in your balloon, let it go, and let the air enter your body, all the air you want. Then breathe naturally. Can you inflate three more balloons?

Now lie back a minute with your back on the mat, bend your knees, and put your hands on your stomach. Do you notice how your stomach rises when you take in air to breathe? Count each time your stomach rises and each time it falls, up to five times. Let's see if you can count five more times. How many breaths can you count without getting distracted?

Now it's time to see how some poses feel.

THE POSES
THE POSES

Tree Pose

Stand on one foot and pretend you are as still as a tree. Focus your gaze on one point and raise your arms as if they were branches. Today you can be a fig tree, with your branches open to the sun, and tomorrow you can be a long, slender cypress that lets itself be swayed by the wind.

What other tree would you like to be?

Do the same thing on your other foot.

Half-Moon Pose

The Moon is a satellite that revolves around the Earth. Did you know that each revolution of the Moon around the Earth takes about one calendar month? The Moon has no light; it reflects the light of the Sun, and depending on how the Sun illuminates it, we see it as full, waning, new, or crescent.

Make a crescent moon with your body. Stand up, stretch your arms over your head with your hands together, and bend very slowly to the left to form a crescent moon. Close your eyes and don't move. Pretend you are the moon in the darkness of the night sky and you light up the room. On what side of your body do you feel more light?

Leave the pose, pause a moment, and before bending to the other side, consider which side of your nose you breathe better with.

You can already do a waning moon!

Cat Pose

Get on your hands and knees and pretend you have a tail like a cat. Without moving either your hands or your legs, start arching your back as if you want to make a very high tunnel. Do you notice how your stomach disappears?

And now the other way around: the tail and the head go up, the chest goes down. The tunnel is upside down!

When you build the tunnel, you release air and meowwwww like a cat. And when you flatten it, you inhale. How many times can you build the "tunnel that meows" without getting tired?

Now think about how cats stretch out by helping themselves with their front paws. Imitate them. Stretch as much as you like—stretch out!

Roaring Lion Pose

First of all, the lion has to concentrate. Sit back on your heels and lift your chest. From your waist up, turn to the left. Look over your left shoulder and relax. Go back to the center, breathe, and slowly do the same to the other side. Look straight ahead again. Think about being a courageous and tranquil lion with a huge heart.

Bend forward slightly and press your hands on your thighs. Raise your chest and lift your heart like a lion sitting on top of a rock. Inhale through the nose, open your mouth, stick out your tongue, and roar like a lion without any fear. Then close your mouth, breathe, and when you have rested, roar again.

Cobra Pose

Lie face down with your hands alongside your chest, and when you're ready, push yourself up with your hands, without bending your knees, like a stealthy cobra. Stay there until you get tired, closely watching imaginary prey. Inhale through the nose and exhale through the mouth making a sssssssssssssss sound, like a hissing cobra. Then rest on the floor like a sleeping cobra.

Tortoise Pose

Now sit on the floor with your legs forward and bend your knees so you can bring the soles of your feet together. Bring your arms under your legs and hold your feet with your hands, on the outside. Pretend that your back is like the shell of a tortoise. It doesn't matter if it's cold or hot, the tortoise retreats into its shell and rests, carefree.

Upside-Down Pose

Reverse the direction of your body. Feet up and head down!

Imagine feet that have eyes, noses, and ears. Feet that look, smell, and listen to what is around them. Feet that take the place of the head, lively and awake, light and happy.

Just Breathe

Now if you like, sit on the floor with your legs crossed. Close your eyes and breathe.

Just one thing.

JUST BREATHE, NOTHING MORE.

Míriam Raventós

I was born in Barcelona, Spain, in 1964. When I was little my mother was already doing yoga, but it seemed a little strange to me . . .

I had to grow up to become interested in yoga, and when I was over thirty I began training to become an instructor. This decision was the start of a very big change. Since then yoga is always with me and helps me live a simple and beautiful life. I'm very grateful for it.

But do you have to be older to discover yoga? No, I don't think that's necessary; that's why I wrote this story.

I studied translation and interpretation in college. Although I studied languages, I'm in love with silence. In silence I feel I'm connected; I never feel alone or isolated.

I live in Bellaterra, Spain, with my children, who come and go, and two dogs who take me for walks in the woods every day. I thank them, too! I like the mountains and music a lot. And I work on different things, some yoga related, such as the management of Proyoga, the yoga studio my mother founded in 1985.

Maria Girón

I was born in Barcelona, Spain, in 1983 and grew up in Garrotxa, Spain (a region of Girona), in a very large, very old house surrounded by trees, the perfect setting for inventing stories and adventures with my brother.

My mother painted and sculpted, and I would sit beside her and watch. Often I would also put my hands to work, and I would draw with the spontaneity of a child that you lose as you grow older. The years passed and little by little I stopped playing, pretending, and drawing.

Until I enrolled in the School of Fine Arts at the University of Barcelona. There I found brushes, painting, and my most creative self again. In my fourth year I went to live in Bologna, Italy, where I discovered printmaking. I spent the following year at the University of Seville, and then I went back to Barcelona and studied illustration at the Llotja School.

I became a mother a little over a year ago, and I illustrated this book bit by bit, taking advantage of all my son's naps.

Original title: *Ioga*. Published for the first time in 2016 in Spain by Fragmenta Editorial.
Copyright © 2016 Míriam Raventós and Maria Girón

Published in the United States of America by
Gibbs Smith
P.O. Box 667
Layton, Utah 84041
Published by agreement with Fragmenta Editorial through the VeroK Agency, Barcelona, Spain.
Copyright © 2018 Míriam Raventós and Maria Girón

Manufactured in December 2017 in Hong Kong by Toppan Printing Co.

First Edition
22 21 20 19 18   5 4 3 2 1

1.800.835.4993 orders
www.gibbs-smith.com

Gibbs Smith books are printed on either recycled, 100% post-consumer waste, FSC-certified papers or on paper produced from sustainable PEFC-certified forest/controlled wood source. Learn more at www.pefc.org.

Library of Congress Control Number: 2017950584
ISBN: 978-1-4236-4935-9